SPACE  OBSERVER

The Planets

by
Jenny Tesar

Heinemann
LIBRARY

First published in Great Britain by Heinemann Library
Halley Court, Jordan Hill, Oxford OX2 8EJ,
a division of Reed Educational & Professional Publishing Ltd

OXFORD   FLORENCE   PRAGUE   MADRID   ATHENS   MELBOURNE
AUCKLAND   KUALA LUMPUR   SINGAPORE   TOKYO   IBADAN
NAIROBI   KAMPALA   JOHANNESBURG   GABORONE
PORTSMOUTH NH (USA)   CHICAGO   MEXICO CITY   SAO PAULO

First published 1997

02 01 00 99 98
10 9 8 7 6 5 4 3 2 1

ISBN 0 431 01459 0

British Library Cataloguing in Publication Data

Tesar, Jenny
    The planets. – (Space observer)
    1. Planets – Juvenile literature
    I. Title
    523.4

This book is also available in hardback (ISBN 0 431 01458 2)
Printed and bound in Malaysia by Times Offset (M) Sdn. Bhd.

Acknowledgments
The publishers would like to thank the following for permission to reproduce
photographs:
Pages 4-5: ©Blackbirch Press, Inc.; pages 6, 18, 22-23: ©NASA/Science Source/Photo
Researchers, Inc.; page 7: A.S.P./Science Source/Photo Researchers, Inc.; pages 8-9,
14: ©Julian Baum/Science Photo Library/Photo Researchers, Inc.; page 10: ©John
Foster/Science Source/Photo Researchers, Inc.; page 11: Gazelle Technologies, Inc.;
page 12: U.S. Geological Survey/Science Photo Library/Photo Researchers, Inc.;
pages 13, 16, 19: ©NASA; page 15: A. Gragera, Latin Stock/Science Photo
Library/Photo Researchers, Inc.; page 17: ©NASA/Peter Arnold, Inc.; pages 20,
21: ©W. Kaufmann/JPL/SS/Photo Researchers, Inc.

Cover photograph: NASA/Peter Arnold, Inc.

Every effort has been made to contact the copyright holders of any material reproduced
in this book. Any omissions will be rectified in subsequent printings if notice is given to
the publisher.

Contents

Some words are shown in bold, **like this**. You can find out what they mean by looking in the Glossary.

The Solar System

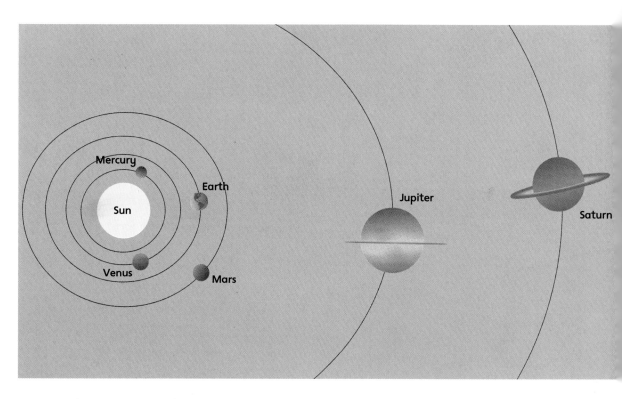

Our solar system has nine planets, including Earth.

Our Earth is part of the Solar System. Solar means sun. The Sun is the centre of our Solar System. The Sun is a huge star.

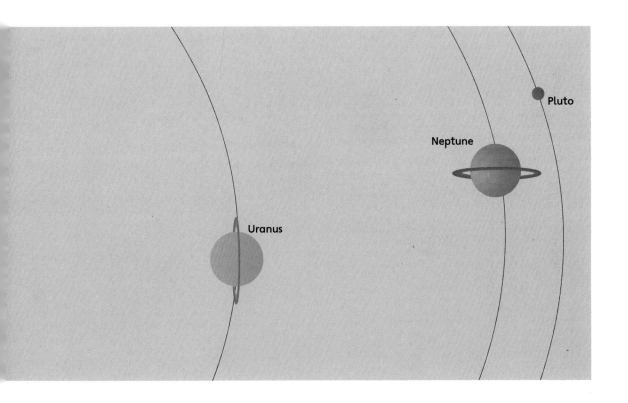

Nine round (ball-shaped) **planets** move in paths called **orbits.** These are like giant ovals around the Sun. Scientists send **probes** to some of the planets to learn more about the Solar System.

Mercury

Distance from Sun: 57 million km
Number of moons: 0
Relative size: eighth largest

Mercury is the closest **planet** to the Sun.
Because Mercury is so close to the Sun, the
side that faces the Sun gets very hot. That
side is much hotter than any place on Earth.

Mercury is closest to the Sun

Mercury's **surface** looks like our Moon

Mariner 10 was a **probe** that visited Mercury. It took hundreds of pictures. The pictures showed that Mercury looks a lot like our Moon.

Venus

Distance from Sun: 107 million km
Number of moons: 0
Relative size: sixth largest

Venus is the second planet from the Sun. It is the closest **planet** to Earth.

Venus and Earth are about the same size. Thick **acid** clouds always cover Venus. People, animals and plants from Earth couldn't live in this **atmosphere**.

More than 20 **probes** have visited Venus.

An artist's picture of one of the 20 probes that have visited Venus

Earth

Distance from Sun: 148 million km
Number of moons: 1
Relative size: fifth largest

Earth is the third **planet** from the Sun. Earth has one **moon**. The moon travels around Earth – at the same time that Earth travels around the Sun.

The moon is always circling Earth

Almost three-quarters of Earth's surface is covered with water

Earth is the only planet with water on its
surface. It is the only planet where there is
known to be life.

Mars

Distance from Sun: 142 million miles
Number of Moons: 2
Relative Size: Seventh largest

Mars is the fourth **planet** from the Sun. It is about half the size of Earth. It has a red color.

Mars is known for its red color.

Mars has large craters shaped like bowls.

Millions of years ago, Mars had water. Today, it is dry. Many scientists think there once was life on Mars. Maybe tiny living things are there today. Two **probes** that arrived in 1997 looked at Mars for signs of life.

Jupiter

Distance from Sun: 774 million km
Number of moons: 16 or more
Relative size: largest planet

Jupiter is the fifth **planet** from the Sun. You could put all the other planets inside Jupiter and still have extra room!

An artist's picture of a **probe** passing a moon on its way to Jupiter

An artist's picture shows Jupiter's rings and some of its moons.

Jupiter is not solid like Earth. It is a huge ball of **gases.**

Six **probes** have already visited Jupiter. They discovered thin rings that circle the planet. Scientists think the rings are made of rocks.

Saturn

Distance from Sun: 886 million miles
Number of Moons: 20 or more
Relative Size: Second largest

Saturn is the sixth **planet** from the Sun.
Like Jupiter, it is a giant ball of **gases.**

Saturn is famous for the beautiful rings
that circle it. The rings are large and flat.

Saturn's rings are made of ice and dust.

A collage showing Saturn and some of its many moons.

They are made of billions of small pieces of ice and dust. Saturn has more **moons** than any other planet. Three **probes** have visited Saturn.

Uranus

Distance from the Sun: 2.7 billion km
Number of moons: more than 15
Relative size: third largest

Uranus is the seventh planet from the Sun.
Like Jupiter and Saturn, it is a ball of **gases**.

Uranus has rings, like the other gas planets.

Uranus is a gas planet with dark rings

An artist's picture shows *Voyager 2* visiting Uranus

Voyager 2 was the only **probe** to visit Uranus. It arrived there in 1986, after visiting Jupiter and Saturn.

Neptune

Distance from Sun: 2.8 billion miles
Number of Moons: 8 or more
Relative Size: Fourth largest

Neptune is usually the eighth **planet** from the Sun. But because of its **orbit,** sometimes Pluto is closer to the Sun than Neptune.

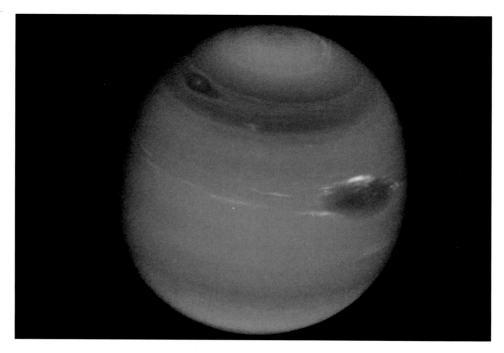

Neptune's rings are too thin to show in this photo.

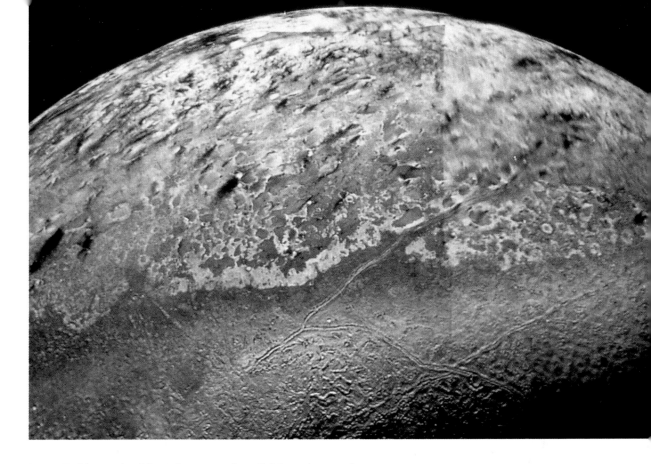

Icy Triton is the largest of Neptune's moons.

Neptune is a **gas** planet and has rings. This planet also has at least eight **moons.** The biggest is Triton. Almost half of Triton is covered with ice. It even has ice volcanoes!

In 1989, *Voyager 2* became the first **probe** to visit Neptune.

Pluto

Distance from Sun: 5.7 billion km
Number of moons: 1
Relative size: smallest planet

Pluto travels in an unusual **orbit** around the Sun. Usually, Pluto is the furthest **planet** from the Sun. But sometimes its path crosses Neptune's path. Then Pluto is closer to the Sun – and Neptune is the furthest planet.

Pluto is a planet made of rocks, not **gases**. It is very cold. Very little of the Sun's heat reaches Pluto.

Pluto has a **moon** called Charon that circles it